I0842513

Also by Ronald W. Kenyon

Divagations: Collected Poetry 1959-1996

A Winter in the Middle of Two Seas: Real Stories from Bahrain

Monville: Forgotten Luminary of the French Enlightenment

Monville: l'inconnu des Lumières (en français)

Le Petit Kenyon: Dining in the Environs of Paris for Walkers

Statues of Liberty: Real Stories from France

On the Trail in France

Floridians: Real Stories from the Sunshine State

Paris Trip Report: Art, Politics, Ale and Motorcycles

Washington City: Real Stories from the Nation's Capital

Saudi Arabia: Reflections of an American

Photography

Metro Portraits

Metro Messages

My Beautiful France

Ile-de-France, terres d'inspiration (en français)

France Images & Messages

ENOUGH!

101 Slogans from the March for Our Lives

Edited by

Ronald W. Kenyon

CreateSpace

2018

First Edition

Preface copyright © 2018 Ronald W. Kenyon
All rights reserved

ISBN-13:9781986936958
ISBN-10:1986936953

In Memoriam

Alyssa Alhadeff

Scott Beigel

Martin Duque Anguiano

Nicholas Dworet

Aaron Feis

Jamie Guttenberg

Chris Hixon

Luke Hoyer

Cara Loughran

Gina Montalto

Joaquin Oliver

Alaina Petty

Meadow Pollack

Helena Ramsay

Alex Schachter

Carmen Schentrup

Peter Wang

PREFACE

A child's life is worth more than all the guns in the world.

The scariest thing in a school should be my grades.

The only thing easier to buy than a gun is a politician.

This book contains 101 of the hundreds of powerful slogans such as the three above that were written on placards, posters and banners and carried on March 24, 2018, during the March for Our Lives, when 800,000 patriotic Americans, students, their parents, their teachers and their supporters, gathered in Washington, DC, in the biggest single-day protest in American history.

The demonstration took place a month after a domestic terrorist massacred 17 innocent teenagers and their teachers at the Marjorie Stoneman Douglas High School in Parkland, Florida, the 30th mass shooting in the first 45 days of 2018.

Millions of supporters gathered in nearly 900 cities all over the United States and in countries from France to New Zealand to Brazil to demand common-sense measures to put an end to the domestic terrorism and mass murder being waged all over the United States on an almost daily basis.

March 24, 2018, is also a date that will be considered as significant as August 28, 1963, when Martin Luther King, Jr. delivered his "I Have a Dream" speech to a crowd of 200,000 assembled on the National Mall in Washington, in which he called for an end to racism and for civil and economic rights. Dr. King's speech resulted in the enactment of the landmark Civil Rights Act of 1964 and the Voting Rights Act of 1965.

Now we are in 2018 and 800,000 Americans demonstrated in the Nation's Capital, demanding that Congress enact gun-control legislation. How long will they

have to wait for Congress to act
and the president to sign a gun-
control bill into law?

I was inspired to compile this
collection because I was reminded
of the student uprising in France
in May 1968. Just as the American
students gave vent to their
imagination in creating the
slogans in this book, the French
students plastered the walls of
Paris with their powerful slogans,
subsequently collected in a little
volume entitled *Les Murs Ont la
Parole*, "The Walls Have the
Floor."

Just as the March on Washington in
August 1966 and the Events of May
in Paris in 1968 sparked action,
the March for Our Lives in March
2018 is sparking similar action.

For example, in an interview with
late-night television host Stephen
Colbert on February 21, 2018, New
York Senator Kirsten Gillibrand
declared that the National Rifle
Association "has a chokehold on
Congress." She continued, "They
have so much power that nothing
was done after Aurora. Nothing was
done after Sandy Hook. Nothing was
done after Charleston. Nothing was

3

done after Las Vegas. And nothing is done now."

Senator Gellibrand elaborated, "It's the power of money. It's the power of communications. It's the fear they instill in Members [of Congress]. And it's morally wrong. The NRA is only concerned with gun sales. It's all about money. It's all about greed. It has nothing to do with the Second Amendment."

The senator boasted that, whereas previously, the NRA had graded her A+, her grade now is an F. She also announced that she has renounced all corporate campaign contributions from any source.

About the same time, *The New Yorker* published in its issue of March 5, 2018, a profile by Mike Spies of Marion Hammer, a former president of the NRA who has been the organization's Florida lobbyist in Tallahassee, the state capital, since the late 1970s.

Although unelected, Hammer exercises more political clout than many elected legislators and even, on occasion, the governor himself.

The influence of this toxic
lobbyist on American society has
been considerable. According to
Spies, "Hammer has shepherded laws
into existence that have
dramatically altered long-held
American norms and legal
principles. She crafted a statute
that allows anyone who can legally
purchase a firearm to carry a
concealed handgun in public."
Similar laws have been enacted in
almost every state.

Hammer also created the country's
first Stand Your Ground self-
defense law: similar legislation
has been enacted in two dozen
states besides Florida, "giving
concealed-carry permit holders
wide discretion over when they can
shoot another person."

As could be expected, the NRA and
the gun worshipers fought back
against the Parkland students and
their 800,000 supporters. CNN
reported on March 28, 2018, that
donations to the NRA tripled after
the Parkland shooting. According
to the Federal Election
Commission, donations to the NRA's
Political Victory Fund tripled

from almost $248,000 in January to more than $779,000 in February.

CNN also quoted the nonpartisan Center for Responsive Politics that the number of people contributing to the NRA in the seven days after the shooting increased almost 500% from the week before. Furthermore, The NRA spent $50.2 million on seven key races during the 2016 election cycle: "The group backed six Republican Senate candidates and, of course, the winning presidential campaign of Donald Trump."

NBC News reported on October 12, 2016, that during the 2016 election campaign the NRA spent more than $21 million to help Donald Trump: $9.6 million on ads and other pro-Trump materials and another $12 million attacking Hillary Clinton.

However, on March 27, 2018, something totally unexpected, a completely unpredictable "black swan event," occurred: retired Supreme Court Justice John Paul Stevens, appointed by Republican president Gerald Ford in 1975, published an op-ed in the *New York*

Times calling for the repeal of the Second Amendment!

Justice Stevens recalled the history of the amendment:

> "Concern that a national standing army might pose a threat to the security of the separate states led to the adoption of that amendment, which provides that 'a well-regulated militia, being necessary to the security of a free state, the right of the people to keep and bear arms, shall not be infringed.' Today, that concern is a relic of the 18th century."

Stevens continued by quoting the late Chief Justice Warren Burger, who was appointed by President Richard Nixon and served from 1969 to 1986. The NRA claimed at the time that federal regulation of firearms curtailed the Second Amendment. Burger denounced the NRA for "perpetrating one of the greatest pieces of fraud, I repeat the word fraud, on the American public by special interest groups that I have ever seen in my lifetime."

Stevens concluded by asserting that repealing the Second Amendment "would honor the memories of the many, indeed far too many, victims of recent gun violence."

To emphasize Justice Stevens's point, the newspaper illustrated the article with a photograph of an 18th century muzzle-loading flintlock musket alongside a 21st century assault rifle.

The following day, Donald Trump tweeted that his administration would never support the repeal of the Second Amendment.

But the students' actions are already achieving positive results: on Friday, March 30, 2018, the Vermont Senate concurred with the Vermont House in approving sweeping gun control measures including a ban on bump stocks, limits on the size of magazines, the expansion of background checks on buyers and the raising of the purchase age for firearms. Vermont Governor Phil Scott declared the following day that he would sign the bill into law.

That is a good start, but is not enough: Vermont is a small state, and anyone who wishes to buy a bump stock, obtain large-capacity

magazines, avoid a background
check or buy an assault rifle at
the age of 18 need only cross to a
neighboring state. The only real
remedy is federal legislation
enacted by Congress and applying
to all 50 states.

So, the battle lines have been
drawn. Whose side are you on, the
side of the NRA and the firearms
industry or the side of the
overwhelming majority of the
American people and their
children?

I am making this collection
available for just $10.00. The
royalties from the sale of this
book will be donated to Everytown
for Gun Safety, the non-profit
organization that advocates for
gun control and against gun
violence. I also encourage readers
to contribute generously to the
Everytown for Gun Safety Support Fund:
https://donate.everytown.org/donat
e/everytown-support-fund.

I would be grateful to readers to
check out my other publications,
listed in the front of this book
and available on Amazon.com, and
purchase anything you find of
interest.

THE
SLOGANS

1791 Called.

It wants its amendment back.

21st Century Weapons: 18th Century Laws

A child's
life is
worth more
than all
the guns in
the world.

Abolish the Second Amendment

Actually,
guns DO
kill people

Am I next?

America,
love your
children,
not your
guns

AR-15s
and GOP
both too
easy to
buy

Are guns
more
precious
than us?

Are your
guns worth
more than
our lives?

Arm teachers with pencils not guns

Armed with ballots

Arms are
for
hugging.
End Gun
Violence.

Being nice isn't bulletproof

Bookbags
not
bodybags

Books
not
Bullets

Bullets Are Not School Supplies

Don't
kill my
future

Duck the NRA.
Damn
autocorrect!

Congress
was afraid
of the NRA.
Now it's
afraid of
teenagers.

Every
day 96
people
die from
gun
violence

Fear has no place in my classroom.

Fire
Congress
not Guns

Girls'
clothing in
schools is
more
regulated
than guns
in America.

Grab 'em by the
the
midterms.

Graduation
not
Graves

Guns
DO
kill
people

Guns don't die.

Guns have
evolved.
The 2nd
Amendment
hasn't.

Guns
will be
the
death of
us.

Hey, hey,
ho, ho, NRA
has got to
go!

Hey, hey,
NRA! How
many kids
have you
killed
today?

I am no
longer
accepting
the things
I can not
change. I
am changing
the things
I can not
accept.

I got an A+
in "Run,
Hide,
Fight,"
because you
got an F in
protecting
me!

I'm a teacher, not a cop.

I should

be

worrying

about my

grades,

not my

life.

I trained to
be a
teacher,
not a
sharpshooter.

I vote for
keeping
guns out of
the wrong
hands.

I want
my kid
to get
A's,
not
PTSD.

I will not
go quietly
back to the
1950's.

I'm not
allowed to
use the
laminator.
You want me
to carry a
gun?

If I die in
a school
shooting,
drop my
body at the
NRA.

If only my
uterus
could shoot
bullets
then I
wouldn't
need
regulation.

If they
survive,
they
will
vote.

If you're
not angry,
you're not
paying
attention.

Isaiah 11:6

...and a
little
child will
lead them.

It
could
have
been
me.

It's
easy.
Buy back
and ban
assault
rifles.

Keep
Me
Safe

Kill
the
Guns

*Konbyen ankò? Poukisa?**

*"How many more? Why?"
(Haitian Creole)

Look into
my eyes and
tell me
that my
life is
worth less
than a gun.

March

&

Vote

Mental
illnesses
are global.
Mass
shootings
are
American.

Money Killed My Friends

My favorite part of the 2nd Amendment is where it says, "Well Regulated Militia"

My life is
more
important
than your
guns.

No Guns
More
Books

No more
silence.
End gun
Violence.

No more
thoughts.
No more
prayers.

Now you've
pissed off
Grandma!

NRA facilitates domestic terrorism.

NRA Get out of Government!

NRA Stop
killing
our kids

NRA: Their Blood Is on Your Hands

Protect Us,
Not Guns

R.I.P.NRA
1871-2018:
"You were
terrible."

Remember
when the
only thing
kids were
afraid of
was a

Pop Quiz?

Respect our
existence
or expect
our
resistance.

Schools are
for
learning,
not
lockdown.

Schools
aren't
shooting
ranges.

Schoolmarms shouldn't be gunslingers!

Stop taking
NRA money!

Straight A's not AK's

Students
today.
Voters in
November.

Teachers
will stand
up to
gunmen, but
Congress
won't stand
up to the
NRA.

Teddy bears
have to
meet
consumer
health and
safety
standards.
Guns don't.

The next
massacre
will be the
GOP in the
mid-term
elections.

The only
thing
easier to
buy than a
gun is a
politician.

"The only
thing that
can stop a
bad guy with
a gun is a
good guy with
a gun," said
the guy who
wanted to
sell two
guns.

"The right
to profit
from the
massacre of
children
shall not
be
infringed."
--NRA

The
scariest
thing in
school
should be
my grades.

This is
a School
Zone not
a
War Zone

This is not
a moment.
This is a
movement.

This is
not
Right or
Left.
It's
Life and
Death.

This
should
have
stopped at
Columbine.

Thoughts
and
prayers
don't
stop
bullets.

Time's up
Congress!
End Child
Sacrifice
by WMD Now!

Too old to
create
change?
Move aside:
we'll do
it.

Vote
spineless
politicians
out!

Say no to
guns.

Washington: the World is Watching

What's
wrong with
background
checks if
you're
innocent?

We march
for our
lives so
that we
don't have
to run for
them.

We want to
read books
not
eulogies.

Who in your
life would
have to die
from gun
violence
for you to
support gun
control?

Why is it
easier to
get a gun
than mental
health
care?

Why is the
NRA more
powerful
than
Congress,
Senate and
our
President?

Yes to
the
Kids.

No to
the NRA.

You can
put a
silencer
on guns
but not
on me.

You
can't
fix
stupid
but you
can vote
it out.

You don't
need a gun
to be
powerful.

2261
June 11, 2022

www.ingramcontent.com/pod-product-compliance
Lightning Source LLC
Chambersburg PA
CBHW051751250726

48659CB00001B/367